KALANI GOES ON SAFARI

KALANI GOES ON SAFARI

WILLOW WILLIS

Copyright © THP KIDS ZONE 2022

County Durham, United Kingdom

The moral right of Willow Willis to be identified as the author of this work has been asserted in accordance with the Copyright, Design and Patents Act of 1988.
All rights reserved. No part of this publication may be reproduced, stored in a retrievable system, or transmitted in any form or by any means, electronic, mechanical photocopying, recording or otherwise, without the permission of the author and copyright owner.
This book is not intended as a substitute or replacement for the advice of counsellors or other professionals. The publisher is not responsible for any goods and/or services offered or referred to in this book and expressly disclaim all liability in connection with the fulfilment of orders for any such goods and/or services and for any damage, loss, or expense to person or property arising out of or relating to them.

ISBN:
978-1-915161-13-0

Tamarind Hill Press
www.tamarindhillpress.co.uk
First published in 2022

Once upon a time, there was a little girl named Kalani.
She liked to learn and was very cheerful like other little girls.

Little Kalani liked to play and have fun, but what she liked most in the whole world was to play with her little dog, Cookie, and her cat, Whiskers.

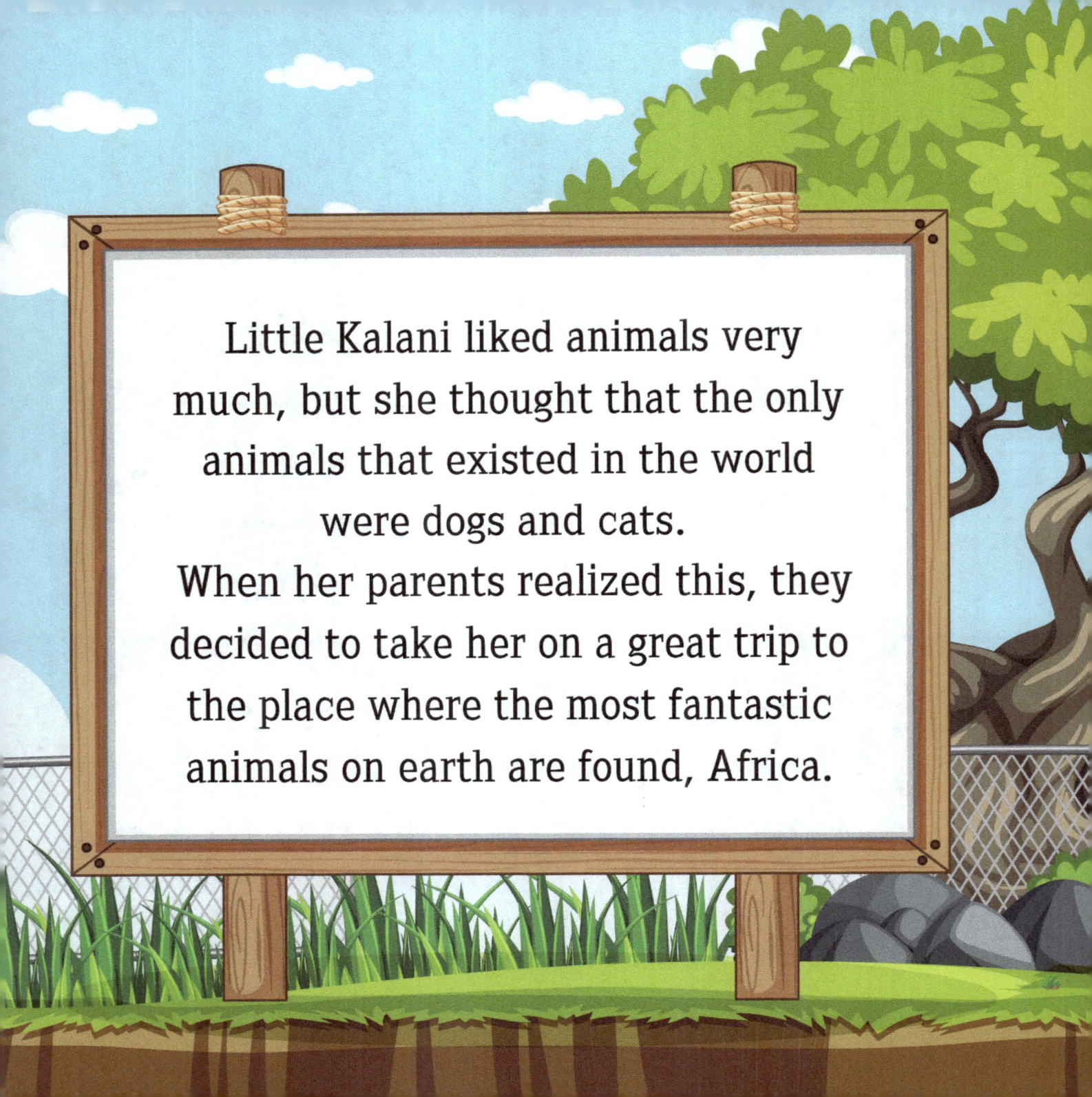

Little Kalani liked animals very much, but she thought that the only animals that existed in the world were dogs and cats.
When her parents realized this, they decided to take her on a great trip to the place where the most fantastic animals on earth are found, Africa.

In Kenya, Kalani and her parents visited a safari. They saw many animals that seemed strange creatures to little Kalani.

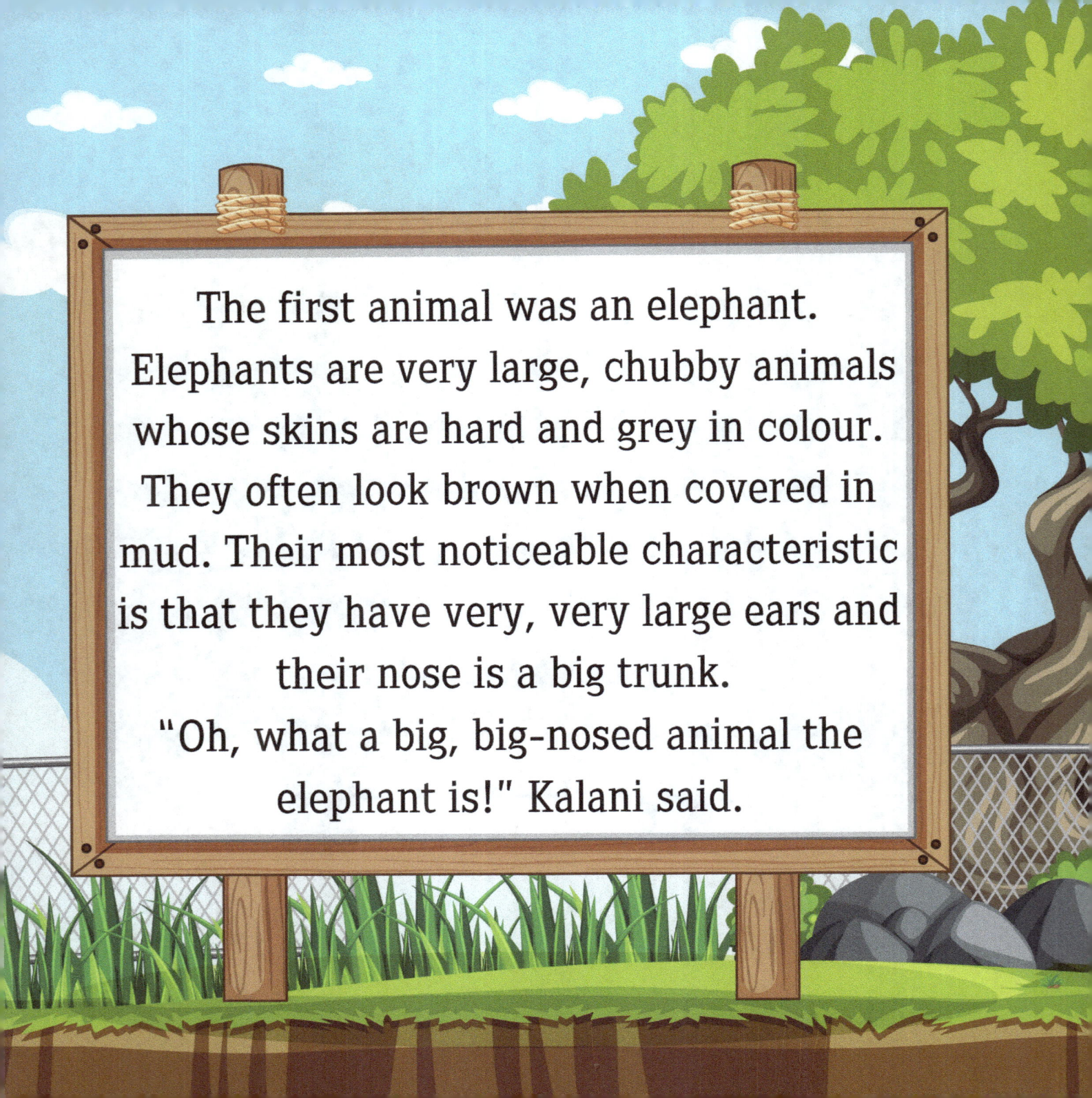

The first animal was an elephant. Elephants are very large, chubby animals whose skins are hard and grey in colour. They often look brown when covered in mud. Their most noticeable characteristic is that they have very, very large ears and their nose is a big trunk.

"Oh, what a big, big-nosed animal the elephant is!" Kalani said.

The next animal they saw was also very peculiar. It was the giraffe.

The giraffe is a very large animal, just like elephants. However, giraffes are very slender. Their bodies are full of dark spots and their most important feature is that they have very, very long necks. It allows them to eat the leaves of the tallest trees!

"How tall giraffes are!" Kalani said. "When I grow up, I would like to be as tall as a giraffe!"

The next animal they saw was very similar to another more common animal, but with much more eye-catching fur. This was the zebra, which is similar to horses and donkeys. However, its most important quality is that it has a coat made of black and white stripes! In addition, zebras always live in herds.
"It would be so much fun to ride a zebra!" Kalani exclaimed.

Then they saw lions! They were very similar to Kalani's cat but much bigger. What impressed the little girl the most were the manes that the male lions had, and she wished she had hair like that too! She heard a roar and suddenly understood why her guide called the lion the king of the jungle.

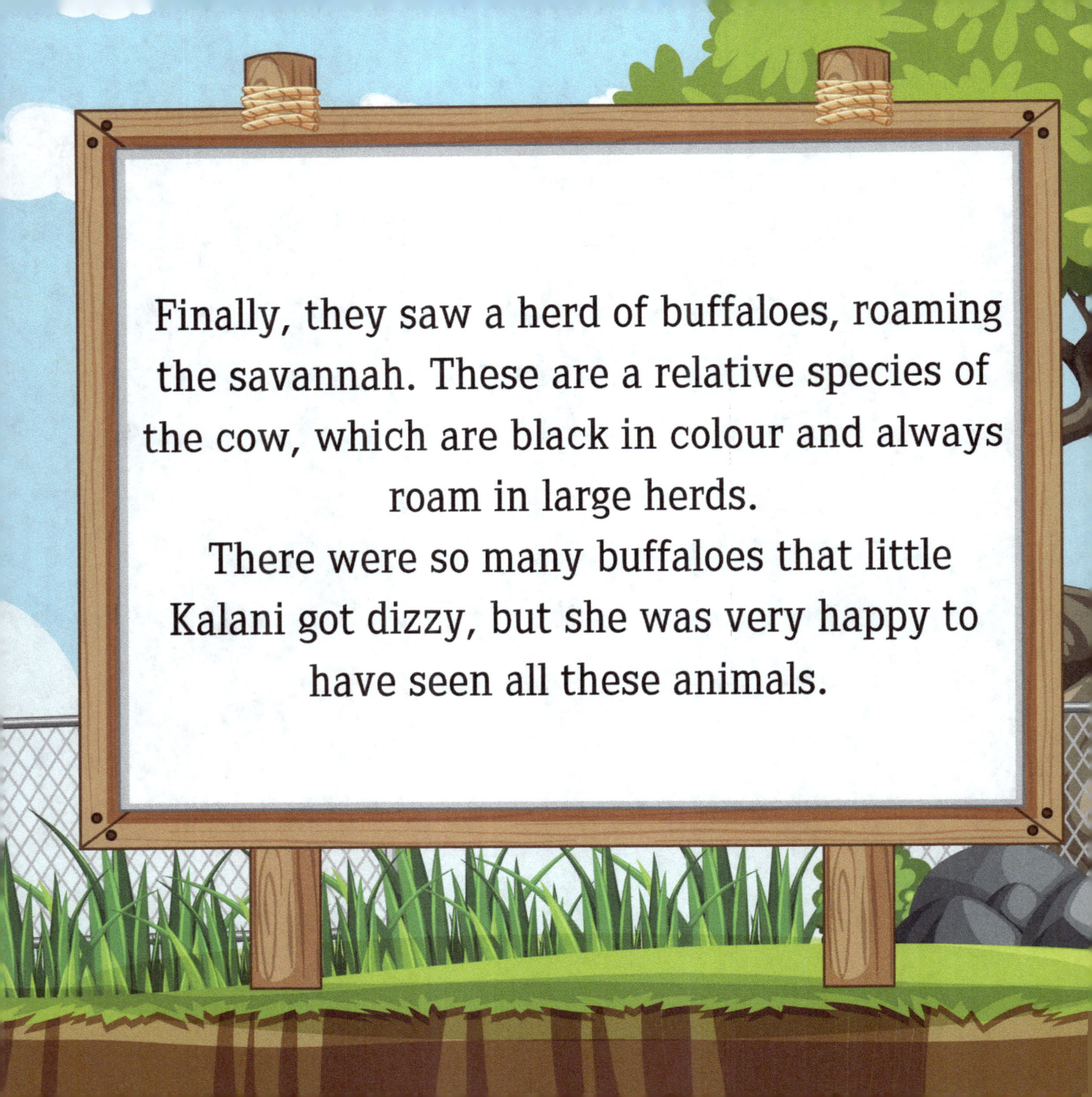

Finally, they saw a herd of buffaloes, roaming the savannah. These are a relative species of the cow, which are black in colour and always roam in large herds.
There were so many buffaloes that little Kalani got dizzy, but she was very happy to have seen all these animals.

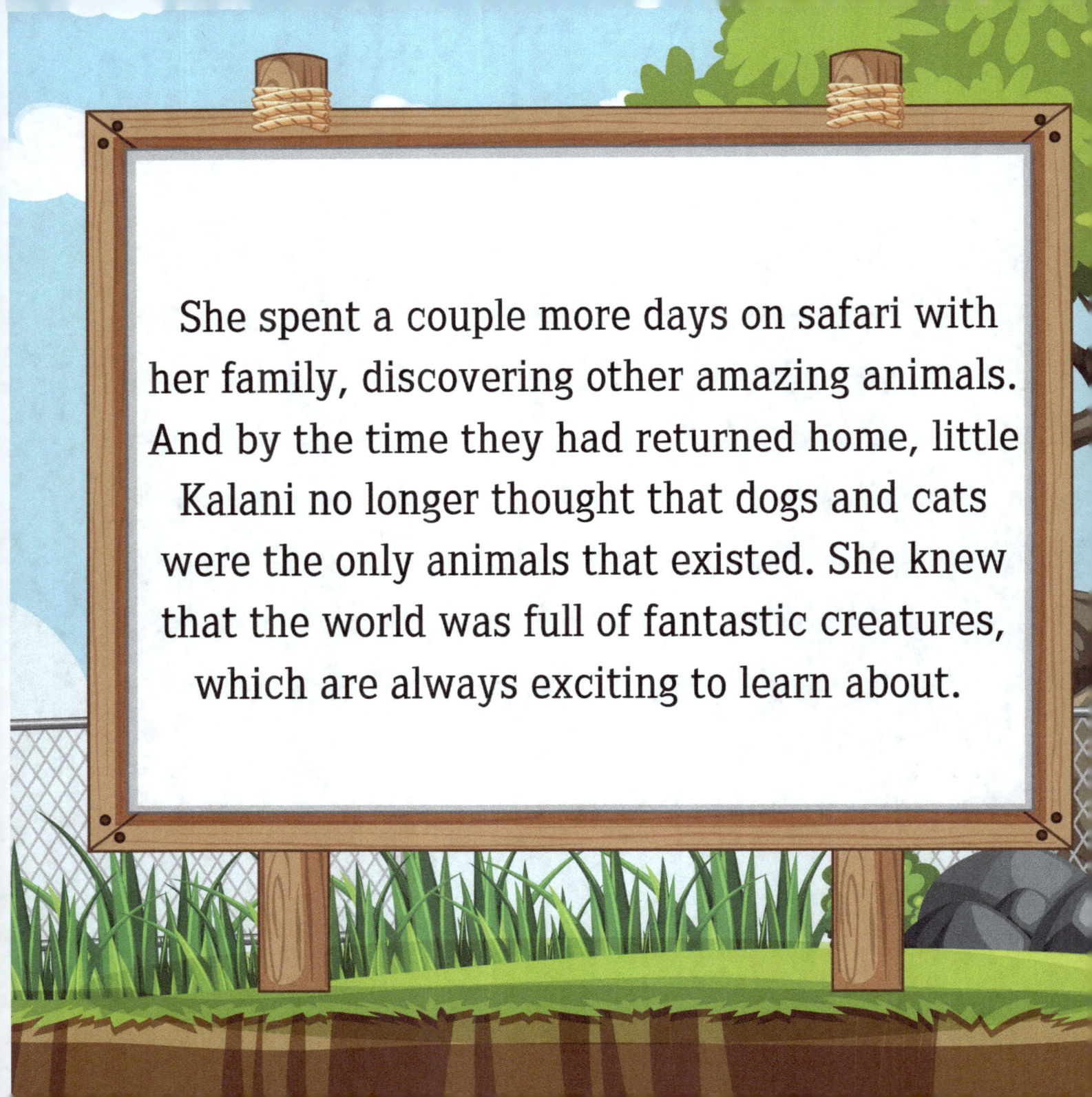

She spent a couple more days on safari with her family, discovering other amazing animals. And by the time they had returned home, little Kalani no longer thought that dogs and cats were the only animals that existed. She knew that the world was full of fantastic creatures, which are always exciting to learn about.

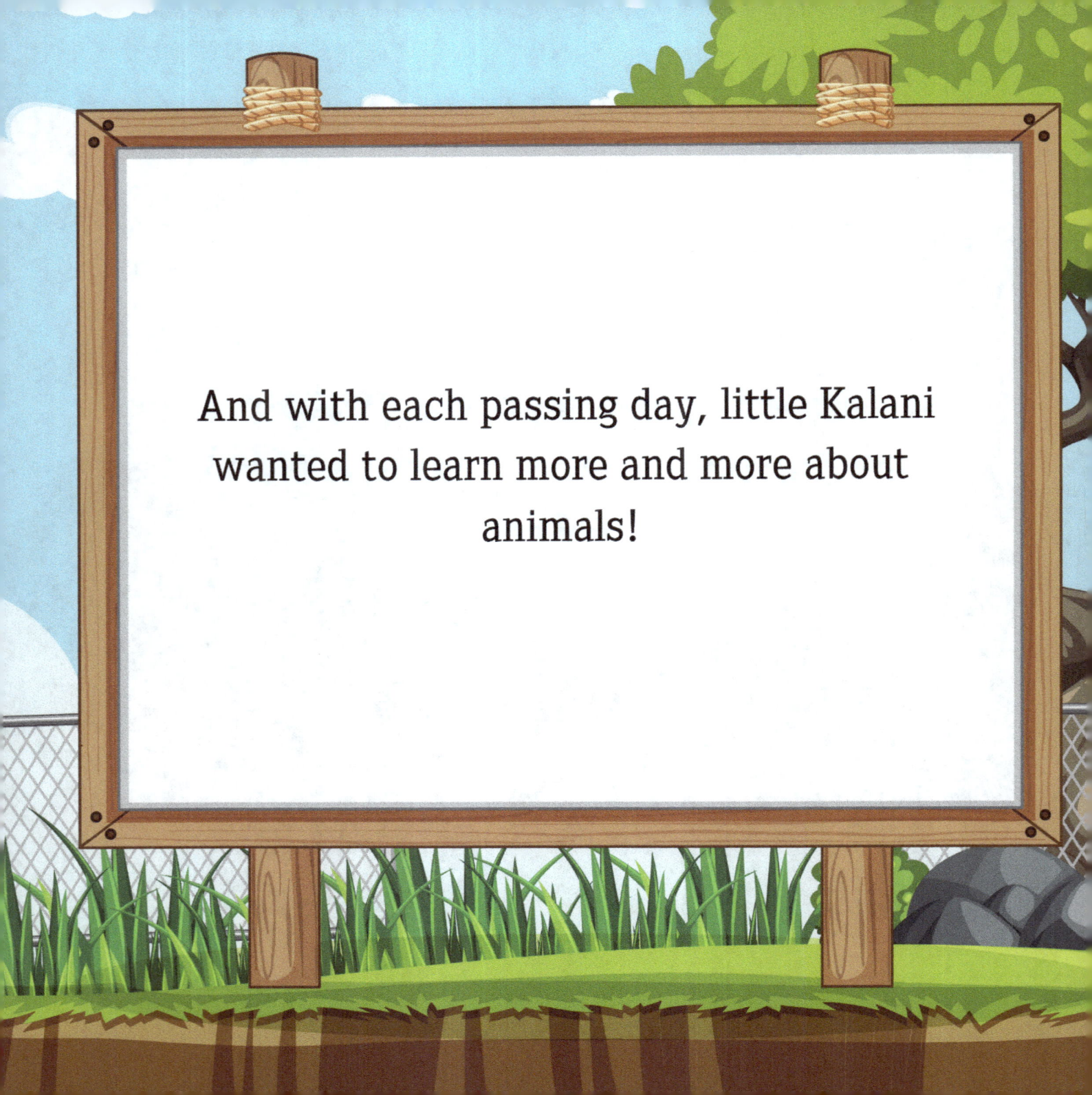

And with each passing day, little Kalani wanted to learn more and more about animals!

This book belongs to:

_____

_____

Published by THP Kids Zone an imprint of Tamarind Hill Press

For Sales and Enquires contact:
Tel: +44 79 82 90 90 37
info@tamarindhillpress.co.uk

www.ingramcontent.com/pod-product-compliance
Lightning Source LLC
Chambersburg PA
CBHW081359080526
44588CB00016B/2541